FAST TALKING PI

FAST TALKING PI

Selina Tusitala Marsh

PUBLICATIONS
2012

Published by Arc Publications
Nanholme Mill, Shaw Wood Road
Todmorden OL14 6DA, UK
www.arcpublications.co.uk

First published in 2009 by Auckland University Press
University of Auckland
Private Bag 92019
Auckland 1142
New Zealand

Design by Tony Ward
Printed in Great Britain by the
MPG Book Group, Bodmin and King's Lynn

978 1904614 35 7 pbk
978 1904614 77 7 hbk

The publishers of this edition would like to express their
thanks to Auckland University Press for all the help they
have given to make the production of this volume possible.

Cover picture: 'Web' by Simon Deighton
© Simon Deighton, 2012,
by kind permission of the artist.

To the ultimate fast talker,
my mother,
Lina Tusitala Crosbie

CONTENTS

Tusitala

Talkback

Fast Talking PIs

All the dark women of history have lost their tongues.
– Yxta Maya Murray, *The Conquest*

be nobody's darling – Alice Walker

TUSITALA

GOOGLING TUSITALA

brings
hotel kitano tusitala dot com
brings
tusitala bar and grill in edinburgh
brings
tusitala built in 1883 scotland
brings
tusitala publishing house a biography of recent
                                        psychodrama books
brings
deviantart tusitala's gallery chicago
brings
tusitala pedigrees for sale – a tibet ansk spaniel, a
                                        japanese chin
8 brings
eBay tusitala year book
19 brings
american idle ask your doctor if its right for you
26 brings
morphology of protozoa, approximately 50 slash long
                                        in *Holomastigoides tusitala*
35 brings
going west festival word of mouth tusitala 11.40–12.00 pm
brings
marinez baldo tusitala karonte strumming a spanish guitar
brings
NZ police news a graduating tusitala constable
brings
the man who was thursday by g k chesterton . . . . truth out
                                        of tusitala spoke dot dot dot
brings
oxford house calendars with tusitala rosy raymond and
                                        storytelling slams

52 brings
the sea slug forum reception at tusitala
56 brings
tusitala a sexydirectory
78 brings
afterlife on tusitala ave with gourmet delights and
freddie mercury
57,092 brings
the tusitala bookshelf in barcelona@bookcrossing.com –
there's no wrong way to eat a rhesus

NOT ANOTHER NAFANUA POEM

Not another nafanua poem she can hear them say as she rides the current of her culture in the new millennium with her electric va'a I'm afraid so her shadow answers back in black but this ride's for nua's sister the one who stayed home and boiled her father's koko alaisa wiping his chin and fetching the key for the cupboard hiding the toilet pepa for the faleuila while her famous warrior sister slays stereotypes on an oceanic scale I'm afraid so because this is the story of how her sister had to replace the stolen coconuts meant for that evening's saka the ones the warrior took without asking to cover her womanhood I'm afraid so because someone had to feed the aiga harvest the kalo the bananas the pawpaw bagging them dragging them to the makeke fou to sell for kupe to pay the government school so the kids can get a scholarship up and outta here so they can come back and open a restaurant in apia and finally begin to lap from those rivulets of glistening stuff gurgling over and into the vaisigano the sewers the streets and the dirt roads of the kua back villages except for nafanua's village someone has to tell said the shadow.

AFAKASI

Half moons ago
people were hollowed-out tablets of stone
spaces were given them
according to spaces they left

some of these spaces were filled with pages
ink leaching out great deeds done
marginalia filled with greater ones

other spaces were filled with fe'e
sliding on story after story
older ones wrapped in thundering fagogo
younger ones rapping ill semantics

other spaces were filled with carved blocks of wood
cocooned in tissue-thin mulberry
these long hollow spaces echoed the beat
of years heavy with folded legs
and the thump thump of old women beating

some spaces were filled with darkness
no light would shine there

other spaces weren't spaces at all
but blistering mirages
no wind would blow there

other spaces were filled with va
these were warmed with the breath of others
the thrum of matua tausi
even if she was just another mirage

other spaces were hard
suffocating stone eyes
calcifying

in other spaces hovered pouliuli
te kore, a nothingness, a yawning galaxy
into these spaces the young would dip their forefingers
rubbing the blackness on their lips
a moko mapping where they had been
and where they were to go

some spaces have pink retro bean-bags in the corner
cups of gumboot tea on the floor
upturned books in punched-out hollows

some spaces are filled
with the music of hands
fa'ataupati, not theatre applause
eyes open, mouths clapped shut
but open-mouthed *choo-hoo! malie!*

some spaces are filled with no dancing
no flying fingers soaring wind
no shuffling of hips
no siva
no tau'olunga
no light in the body

some spaces are tied with rubber bands
trying to render control over
black unruly spaces
a parting and a plaiting of space
a twisting of space into a bun

some spaces are filled with sunlight soap
from the kagamea
laughing over rocks into the ocean
where a dead Alsatian floats under a net of flies
caught underneath the makeke pier

some spaces are brown
some are blue
o lo'u igoa Tusitala
je m'appelle Marchant
flow in and out
turning space sinopia

CALABASH BREAKERS

we all know
the calabash breakers
the hinemoas
the mauis
the risk takers
the younger brother
the only sister
the orphan
the bastard child
with rebellious blood

we all know
the hierarchies
the tapu
the boundaries
always crossed
by someone
petulant

we all know
the unsettled
the trouble makers
the calabash breakers
they sail the notes of our songs
stroke the lines of our stories
and reign in the dark hour

we should know them
we now need them
to catch bigger suns

HONEH SAID

chris abani
said
hone said
the only land I am
is that between my toes
but anne read
that hone said
the only land I have
is that between my toes
then michele said
selwyn said
hone had said

which is why
chris had written

it's the difference between
being
and owning
surging
and standing
living
and landing
she said
she'd read
he said
have
not am

I keep
the am
anyway

then ken said
ron mason said
it first

THINGS ON THURSDAYS

If Updike could do it
why couldn't she?

Surely the forest of books
the cropped rows of frames
lining his house
shouldn't make that much difference?

Surely if he can rent a one bedroomer in Paris
clear his schedule
six mornings a week
and write
publish a novel
five days after each child's birth
be inspired by his wife's art
and write
travel to Rio de Janeiro one week
Geneva the next
and write
pick up a baby
smell her neck
and write
feed the rabbit
watch it jump and run
and write
teach and read
prop up solid oak lecterns
argue with publishers
move house four times
and write
be acclaimed
and famed
and write

wipe the literary slate clean
and write
drop off famous writers
pick up famous painters
add an extension to the house
to write
and write
do parent-father things on Thursdays
and write
speak for money
write for money at *The New Yorker*
and write
enthuse over critical reviews
and Burt Britton's drawings
and write
why couldn't she?

She just needed to
clear the sink
wipe the bench
and write
be inspired by encrusted cups
and write
travel with the vacuum down the hall
into four bedrooms
and write
pick up the kids from school
and write
publish school walking bus committee notices
and write
be inspired by an overgrown lawn
and write
teach and read

to the kids
pick up a baby
smell her neck
and write
change the baby
feed the baby
watch him jump and run
and write
prop up the finances
argue with the parking warden
move house four times
and write
exclaim and rage
and write
wipe the baby tip to toe
and write
drop off the DVDs
drop off the school-age kids
pick up groceries
add a second washing line
and write
be parent-helper on Thursdays
and write
work for money twice a week
6 am to 9 pm
and write
enthuse over her son's stories
the other son's drawings
and write
wash bath and feed
and write
clean out the fridge
in the closet

behind the couch
and write
disinfect the toilet
find the missing rolls
get the rego and WoF
and write
read for work
and write
write for work
and write
work to write

yeah right

SONG FOR TERRY

I stretched into a song
with sun playing the body
long and caramel
in the kitchen Anne's
popping sing bubbles
away
rewind/stop/play
I am her hi-fi audience
offering ears for binding
by the chords in her throat
she is every mean chant
every highfaluting prayer
every ululating bass guitar
every saxophone soliloquy
she is an orchestra
calling to arms those
brave enough to sing
meaty in the delight their fingers
press from each HB'd chord
stop / rewind
she chants while I sauté
gravy beef, onions, garlic
a little olive oil
she chants while I cook vermicelli
I cut while translucent chords float
inflecting the water
bubbling its song on the Atlas
the sun bends the chord
and Anne begins to boil
I chant with my fingers
knead words like
kalino kalinche
and purple sky woman

into the dough
slap spoons stirring soy sauce into sapasui
and who would ever know
that his pancreas is dying
most painful when lying on his back
most tiring at one after noon
but he can still make a poem sing
at four in the morning just after
he tap tap taps out morphine
chanting its numbers down throat to brain
the chemicals meet, the notes blend
a pathway shuts down
two lines descend just before
sleep sings in numbered days
stop / fast forward
I stretch into a song
of my unmaking
the children laugh at Anne's American drawl
her hymns blow the blinds inside out
they wink knowing some secret song is being sung
her growling bass peels the tiles
off the floor
skews the clock
and tilts the colander off balance

I turn the volume down
as the in-law comes to check
that the pot is still round
the stove still square
the bubbles from the sapasui
the correct spherical dimensions for grandchildrenly
                                        consumption
and above all that they do not sing when they pop

stop
Anne's a witch
the Bible says
a blaspheming, hedonistic ranter
play
a mother, a singer
a fast speaker
I say
yawning away the in-law
and making a singular stretch towards that sun
it shook from me a hip
then another
then plucked a twirl
sounded a clap
a jump
then hearing the music of mother's body
the children ra ra ra-ed around the kitchen table.

LANGSTON'S MOTHER

you sd

    get up

        life ain't no crystal stair

                climbed up out of
                       there

    rose

I heard

CARDBOARD CROWNS

morning

I'm with
eighteen year olds
we talk about the crisis
in NZ lit
and the problem of reading
like
they don't

there's a fictional yawn from the back

their books weigh down
their bodies not their minds

afternoon

I'm cooking with five year olds
sculpt flour, yeast, water
mozzarella fingers dip and rise

I keep an eye
on my new starter
his bony body
under an over-confident uniform

he's educating me
in bravery

yesterday

I'm baking a cake and roasting a chicken
simultaneously

blowing up gold balloons
taping them to the king's throne
a creased kindy hat becomes a tama aiga crown
as green spears fan between toetoe heads
over a crayoned five

kids said the chicken was good
it tasted like cake

today

the eighteen year olds buzz over
Wendt's 'Robocop in Long Bay'
theory pop pops the air
V guarana cans
moor the tables
as the book floats away

I throw out a life line
but no one's read it

tomorrow

the five year olds
are Tagaloa's boat builders

o le tala i tufuga o le vaa o Tagaloa

they stomp-sing, pull
fell and gnaw with their teeth in the dark
till they see the dawn

they know when to hide
they've all read the story

THE SUM OF MUM

she begins to calculate:

that's 3 times 9 months
that's 3 times (approximately 30 days times 9)
which is really 3 sons times 270 days
equals 810 days of combined incubation
that's 24 hours a day
equals 19,440 hours of combined incubation
but one came early
one month early
so minus one set of 30 days
equals 810 minus 30 equals
780 days times 24 hours a day equals
18,720 hours of combined incubation

when the sons floated in her universe
yolk eyes staring into membrane galaxy
flicking pulse and finger
nail into red-darkness
she breathed for all of them
always will because
everything adds up to four

WILD HORSES

for Paula

there's chewing gum
on *wild horses*
at the corner of Kitchener
and Victoria and I wait every day
hostage to the adolescent man
his evanescent grin

he used to shout
but lost his voice under foot
of rain, wind, sun and bird

I've already heard what you have to say

nudging the sunglasses higher
the ear-piece further in a window
there's a sculpture on the street
a flickering hubcap
a woman's peeling heel
gutter chatter and
that piece of gum
again
his voice rises
from the hum of the city's throat

I'm held by a red man
riding wild horses again

THREE TO FOUR

a red whistle
is fingered
twice a day
once, just after she pulls on
a heavy winter jacket
in January
and once,
to anchor her frame
to the car
so she won't drift away
on the tarmac
back to Avondale

he puffs his cheeks and blows
soars with the squeal of it
red plastic birdsong leaving him
chanting for breath

as she did
heaving him into the light

that shrill
like the cry of a broken tui
the skidding of a tyre
corner of a day-care
fender of a Ford
tuffs of hair in the grill

that shrill
a feral cat in her throat
as Ford is sentenced six for his four
and out in three

Le Amataga
THE BEGINNING

t a l o f a   A l
m a l o   l a v a   f o r
l e   a m a t a g a
a first in the land
o f c a n n e d a l o h a
I r e m e m b e r o '
neil street and manoa
a p a r t m e n t p o r t a l s
p   o   u   l   i   u   l   i
between the door-jambs
p e l e ' s f i e r y h a i r
over bookshelves steam
the glass of pule's
s i g n e d h a l a h a l a
the pathway is clear
for the child to be
b   o   r   n
that was for your
m o k o p u n a f r i e n d s
lone coffee sippings
sometimes a student
b e a r i n g a *w a i h e k e*
g u l f n e w s-w r a p p e d
s   n   a   p   p   e   r
but this is different
this is space finger
tongue pointing to void
drawing in each eye
b   l   a   c   k
stars tail spinning
the night flashing in
z e r o   d e n s i t y

drawing in every
other mattered thing
c o n g r a t s
on taming in gasps of blood
in breaths of yellow moons
and black holes exhale
when we came that day
micah's favourite shone
azure shimmers of
t   e   m o a n a
n u i   a   k i w a
where frigate bird waves
pulled sky into sea
he swam indigo
ua sua mai le tai taeao
ua a'e i lagi le gogosina
the morning high tide
c o m e   g o g o s i n a
f   l   y
to the heavens
his malaga starts
tunnelling through whirl
pools stargates flicking
out comet words fall
burning canvas floors
when the others left
w h i l e   w e   a t e
r   e   i   n   a   '   s
sweet poke and sea
weed he was the one
to see the sweeter
s   e   c   r   e   t

flashing out
a tongue to taste it
sliding his finger
down cerulean
valleys of pele the
w   o   r   d
blood pricked trace
her stardust tail calls
e   pele   e
e   pele   e
e   pele   e
that's how I found
him fishing acrylic
o   c   e   a   n
hauled up on
manoa's reef locks
p   e   l   e   '   s
lava black matting his
fingers wish we could
be at louis pohl's
palm beach's red
shed will have to do
m   i   c   a   h   '   s
saturn magenta
rings blaze black
on black on a 5 x 5
canvas small enough
to pocket but large
enough to burn
h   o   l   e   s

SPARE THE ROD

That kid
his body
a semi-buried petroglyph
a prehistoric flyer
soaring over stones
or one of those beached sea-birds
washed up
beyond death
finely picked bones
an elegant ivory
sucked clean by ocean's teeth
a polished
egg-shell
opaque without
flesh or feather
trialled by sun and wind
sentenced to freedom

A SAMOAN STAR-CHANT FOR MATARIKI

fetu tasi

I call forth Mata Ariki, the Eyes of God
to watch over Papatuanuku and her people
I call forth wishes for the new June moon
spoken in shadow corners
steaming in palmy places

fetu lua

I call forth the pickled eel in brine
lolling like tongues of story
let loose under a feasting sky
I call forth the moki and korokoro
to fatten nets
that they might feel the weight
of wealth in giving

fetu tolu

I call forth matariki ahunga nui
the overturning of the earth
the bearing of new seedlings
I call forth the kumara and kalo
rooting in fanua for this divine moment
of cyclic beginnings
I call forth the planting of all things
fresh in the soil of the mind

fetu fa

I call forth the pákau
the six-tailed kites
to tickle the heavens
make us laugh
I call forth kite bulging with treasures
woven histories pressed
and plaited by kuia thumb

fetu lima

I call forth the smaller hand
unfurling in the bigger
whanau spiralling like
an unfathomable prime
I call forth the harvesting of whakapapa
the sowing of blood lines
the clearing of weeds from graves
the tihei in that first born breath

fetu ono

I call forth the knotting of star-charts
by sinnet and shell
I call forth the vaka and all manner of vehicle
navigating by our light
into the long safe journey home
into the uncharted night

fetu fitu

I call forth the rising of my six sisters
in Ranginui's pre-dawn cloak
I call in greeting
talofa mata ali'i
ia orana matarii'i
aloha makali'i
kia ora matariki
I call forth the music of bone flutes
the chant, the song, the karakia
guiding the traveller's feet
and heavenward eyes

CIRCLE OF STONES

Fale Pasifika, Tamaki Makau Rau

for once let the children ask their fathers for food
let the students argue points of view with someone else

for once let policy and poetry analyse itself, even
the novel can write itself home tonight, for once let's sit

for this is no ordinary slab, no ordinary circle
we are seated on Hawaiki, its basalt of death and birth

in this space of ancient vigil, we watch our children grow
in this space of initiation, our hands grant us entry

sowing konai weaves kakala of royal
heilala, langakali scents us

reaping sia's moreton bay fig becomes
banyan, wrapping roots round her moon circle

sowing momoe cuts ruby into limestone, twisted
hem of heart wrung from iron hands

reaping karlo's ta'ovala swoops the keyboard
smearing screens in dark chocolate

sowing marilyn inks an ipu ava tips
a libation and drinks niu voices

reaping serie dyes siapo the colour of fagogo
flying, they nest in a westie pulu tree

sowing luamanuvao bypasses the beehive
going west to link arms with poetry

reaping tusiata steps off a plane, Nafanua
by her side, te moana nui breaking on their lips

sowing grace places black stone in the middle
its glass cuts the living, embedding the obsidian night

reaping alice piles a stone on a stone on a stone for those
to come, makes slings for those who don't want them to

sowing jully takes the tide and fills the circle saying
it's what doesn't get washed away that counts

reaping teresia marks a map, Nei Nim'anoa
sets it on water, their stone becomes a vaka

sowing misatauveve lays the thirteenth, the letters
'P' 'A' arc and disappear under fale belly, over the Pacific

in Poutūterangi's light I throw a calabash high
stone shadows watch it plummet through sky and
smash

cupping our hands we catch the seeds

TALKBACK

GUYS LIKE GAUGUIN

I

thanks Bougainville
for desiring 'em young
so guys like Gauguin could dream
and dream
then take his syphilitic body
downstream to the tropics
to test his artistic hypothesis
about how the uncivilised
ripen like pawpaw
are best slightly raw
delectably firm
dangling like golden prepubescent buds
seeding nymphomania
for guys like Gauguin

II

thanks Balboa
for crossing the Isthmus
of Panama
in 1513
and pronouncing our ocean
the South Seas
hey thanks, Vasco
for making us
your underbelly
the occidental opposite of all
your nightmares
your waking dreams
inversion of all your laws
your darkest fantasies

thanks for seeing the earth as a body
the North, its head
full of rationality
reasoned seasons
of meaning
cultivated gardens
of consciousness
sown in masculine
orderly fashion
a high evolution
toward the light

thanks for making the South
an erogenous zone
corporeal and sexual
emotive and natural
waiting in the shadows
of dark feminine instinct
populated by the Africas
the Orient, the Americas
and now us

NAILS FOR SEX

They started stealing iron
from the *Dolphin*

when the trade supply
ran aground

dismantling beams
loosening boards

save for punctuating
mast shocking the air.

The captain lost control
as discipline warped

fissuring under
wrecked deck planks

moaning holes where nails had
once fixed them proper for sex.

MUTINY ON PITCAIRN

for Jenny

I will build a boat
I will leave this island
these seasaltmen
forcing us to be with them
then others

I will build a boat
leave this island
these mutineers who think they can
live paradise
on this land
kill my men
and be done

I will build a boat
and the name of Tēhuteatuaonoa
shall flood their ears
then the world will know
we did not go
without
building boats

TWO NUDES ON A TAHITIAN BEACH, *1894*

Gauguin,
you piss me
off.

You strip me bare
assed, turn me on my side
shove a fan in my hand
smearing fingers on thigh
pout my lips below an
almond eye and silhouette me
in smouldering ochre.

I move
just a little
in this putrid breeze
hair heavy to
fuscous knees, still
I'm the pulse
on the arm of this wall
and I've drawn her to me again.

Here she comes.

Not liking that she likes me
not liking you, but knowing that she
likes me, not liking you
liking me, but she
likes me and sees me,
but not you,
because you
Gauguin,
piss us
off.

VENUS IN TRANSIT

for Rowan

To Romans she was Venus
     Queen of sea
     wringing pleasure from opalescent hair.

To Cyprians
     she was Atargatis of Askalon
     Queen of mermaids
     in her wake
     dolphins arc through fecund seas.

To Aeneas she was Aphrodite
     born fully formed
     from Aegean sea in a *kteis*
     flesh in a scallop shell.

To Rowan
     she was Venus in transit
     no Botticelli birth
     but a Ma'ohi insurrection
     hair scalloping midnight trades

     an inflamed scarlet hibiscus
     undoing the Florentine gaze of her sister
     her right hand speaks of many sisters
     blue-black webbing bear

     the lines of Tahiti's tupuna vahine
     on the *Bounty*
     on the cover her left hand
     has crossed over the border.

REALPOLITIK

In 1776 there was no God past Cape Horn
civilised Christian men
left their breeches
belts and boots
hanging on trees
as they headed
for Paradise

Otahitie

Garments were gathered
on return
so waiting wives
could wash them whale tooth white.

A woman for wifely purposes
could be found among the Cape Colony Dutch
freshly risen loaves and hearty stews
laundered children blue eyed
like their fathers –
but for spice
a woman from Tahiti
could be made
wife for a few
moons, a blade or two.

Apparently Cook tried really hard
                we interduce among them wants
in 1778
                and perhaps diseases
in Hawai'i
                which they never before knew
not to spread

his crewmen's cock and ball
distemper
syphilis
VD
& which serves only to disturb
among the natives.

Apparently, he tried
that happy tranquillity
really
they and their fore Fathers
really
had injoy'd
hard.

CONTACT 101

the philosopher gazes
sets eyes on purity and the ease of it
the landed naturalness of
thigh, rump, curvature of spine
buttock her Venus torso
and says
      see there
           see her
                see the uncorrupted cave

the scientist stares
notes the unnaturalness and the disease of it
power, autonomy, to cry, to feel, to love truly
beyond the bounds of her polygenic body
and says
      see there
           see her
                see the furious womb

the anthropologist peers
sees her animality
the languishing exotic, the dying race
and says
      see her
           see them
                see us in all our glory

HAS THE WHOLE TRIBE COME OUT FROM ENGLAND?

ask the Aurora, the Duchess of Argyle, Jane Gifford
ask the Westminster, the Bangalore, the Ramillies
ask Sir Robert Sale, William Bryan, Amelia Thompson
ask the Timandra, the Blenheim, the Whitby
ask Will Watch, the Arrow, the Fifeshire
ask Lord Auckland, Mary Ann, the Victory
ask the overcrowded Lloyds where 65 perished
ask St Pauli, the Skiold, Philip Laing, John Wickliffe
ask Blundell and Bernicia, the Chelydra
ask Charlotte Jane, Randolph, Sir George Seymour
ask the Cressy, the Fly, the Castle Eden
ask Isabella Hercus, and Travancore
ask the 12,000 miles of sea
ask

      the dead

            babies

ask

      the new ones

ask
and ye shall receive

a year and 9000 settlers later

Wellington is no longer
a question

WHAT'S SARONG WITH THIS?

for Sima

Moran and his Pineapple Peauties!
Honolulu Honeys
Moore's Hollywood Broads playing South Seas Native
plaster the Tiki Bar
Vargas and Elvgren
wahine artists presenting
the '40s, '50s and '60s
to foreign lips
licking both sides of the black velvet divide
(L) unknown (C) (not a Leeteg)
Image at (R) is film actress Gene Tierney
is film actress Debra Paget
is a film actress

Medcalf Thompson MacPherson Randall Defeltson

Are You In Favour Of This Motion?
hips lips belly-buttons swirling see-through skirts and
nipple leis
A Fair Bit of Peekabooin' Goin' On There!
hibiscus lavalava wrapped tight
clit butt boobs plumped cupped and dished on palms
milky south seas kitten
climbs a coconut tree
straddling its ridges
drinks from a plucked nut
keeping her sunset sienna high heels on
like the trunk, her toes bow
artists Earl and Bill and their calendar ma'ams
reddy lipped pointy titted mouths agape in song
this one balances a basket on her head
à la Caribbean

a banana pokes her chin
makes her grin and wink
and say
Fit To Be Tied!
Look Out Below!
I Hope The Boys Don't Draw Straws!
Aloha oooohhhh aaaahhhh!
What's Sarong With This?
that one fingers a ukulele
lies on her back
pins in the air
90 degrees
ankles primly crossed
while thighs like freshly peeled mangoes
quiver and
Man Goes Alright!
this brunette prowls
more sober than the blonde
that one is wild and panty free
bronco bucking her body
this one's bottom peeks through
a dusky made-in-Taiwan grass skirt
Vargas' one balances on tiptoes
while hanging a lei
her wrap rides up from the effort
Does it? doe-eyes say
that one lifts her bronze mane from a sweaty neck
ribs jut below dew-drop breasts
the last one kneels before an over-sized tiki
jokes like smoke hang heavy
in the beer-breath bar

Are All These Honeys Making You Hungry?
Try Some Hula Apples
Distributed by Universal Fruit and Produce Co. Seattle, Wash.
One Volume Bushel
Product of USA

the half-caste arches her back
pulls up her knees
hulas
pours a gourd of water
over her breasts
snaps castanets
naked
a volcano erupts in studio moonlight
posies sway at her feet
while weaving a lei
climbing a tree
lying on leopard skin
biting throated pearls
while wrap is ripped by Saint Bernard
forgetting it's slipping
finding herself shockingly
all breasts belly fanny
while prowling across the floor
exposing her neck
to an anglo kiss
his anglo embrace
round her six-inch anglo waist
as he thumbs
the 's' of her spine
her bared toes
like his lip, curl

Miss Half-caste is crowned
Miss Aloha
Miss Tropicana
Miss Tutti Frutti
Miss Bunnypants
and gets to keep
the velvet sash

THE CURATOR

the artist from Holland
specialised in fat-bellied mamas
fat finger-tipped big-lipped mamas feeting the fat-bellied
                                                        earth
like freshly muddied spuds sunning themselves
                                            through the dirt
a kete of purpling kumara
freshly baked from her palette
simmered in browns and aubergines
seared in floral Hubbards
cooled with fanning hands
in a shadowless land
that Dutch lady sure can paint

the poet from Pasifika
canvases letters in monochrome
light plays on every rounded vowel
chiaroscuro on every line
stanzas of rhythmical heat
painted with sepia-spoken brush
blurring black white history often

she waits at bus stops
spills words on Starbucks serviettes
creased Fullers pamphlets
expired diary days
marking the dark jogger's dream

the curator suggests she read
one of her nicer poems
something apropos of an opening
some thing to go with the feta and hummus
meatballs he says as he hangs up a space between them
and marvels at the divide

HAWAI'I: PRELUDE TO A JOURNEY

for Haunani-Kay

you go then
poppin' in bubble-gum jeans
you, wrapped bubble-gum teen
knowin' nothin'
'bout no Hawaiians
not living
in Waikiki
no more

you go then
floating on two-buck sunshine
courtesy of Longs
one of a dozen stores stacked
against a postcard beach
within reach of King Kamehameha's
you surface from under the slick of tourist

you go then
buy five key rings for ten
two hibiscus singlets for one
free Hershey bars softening in the sun of
Aloha Stadium fermenting
red-tipped toes in jandals
pale chests in floral shirts
necks noosed in fluorescent lei
wrists handcuffed in gold, etched with black enamel
detained by Reebok and Nike

you go then
to finish in Hale Manoa
where student voices
rise above smoking black bean stir-fry

fa'alifu fa'i, tofu and udon noodles
breezing open pavilions
you go then
to class to find friends
kama'aina who surf and protest
he is writing on Hawaiian land rights and kalo
sings at the Royal Hawaiian
for his fees
she is writing on post-'80s sovereignty
like waves lapping a broken shore
we are one we
are more she writes
he is writing on wipe-outs of Kamehameha Schools
surfs Sunset
always goes for the barrel
no matter how he gets worked

you go then
and meet
Pele's pen
her black ink lava
ever pricking the night

you go then
to hula halau to
the picket sign to the
angry line outside parliament to
Greevy's photo exhibition to the
kalo plantation to
the valley of stolen waters to the
valley of ground bones and mortar to

the majesty of Kilauea
you go then
smell embered Lincolns
wrapped in kalo leaves
wedged in creases
of Pele-'ai-honua
eater of the land

looked in the crowd
for you peered in every face
even asked twice
at the door for you

mute
they pointed to the second floor

I found the theodores and the roberts
the george henrys, renés, and augustes
the huberts, the charles, and james
the jules, the enochs, the alexanders
the ambroses, mabels, cornelias
and the juliettes, madges, and keichis
the satorus, lloyds, and toshikos
the tadashis, the jacques and the louis
cramming walls of rooms
dedicated to you

but until the
hand-made stitching
red white blue
four flags
a flowering crown
I did not see you

some artists earned space
by living in Hawai'i a year
those in silent stitching
were here a thousand

ALICE'S BILLBOARD

indians discovered
columbus burn this

CD responses to oct 15
emergency security call

463 8888 48 hours of
movie madness cornell

university founded AD
1865 sex and the city

indigenous literatures
and the arts howl if you

love city lights books
pacific worlds and the

american west I
THINK therefore I'm

dangerous women in
grad school . . . women of

valour american aloha
hula beyond hawai'i

powell's the legendary
independent bookstore

toonahowi and
tomo-chi-chi

FAST TALKING PIs

FAST TALKIN' PI

for Anne Waldman

I'm a fast talkin' PI
I'm a power walkin' PI
I'm a demographic, hieroglyphic fact-sheetin' PI

I'm a theorising PI
I'm a strategising PI
I'm a published in a peer reviewed journal PI

I'm a slot machine PI
I'm a lotto queen PI
I'm tote-ticket church bingo TAB PI

I'm a vegan PI
a rainbow warrior PI
I'm a protest sign against the rising waters PI

I'm a criminal PI
behind the bar graphs PI
I'm a gun smokin' patching totin' king cobra PI

I'm a fale PI
I'm a marae PI
I'm a living breathing dwelling of my ancestors PI

I'm a lazy PI
I'm a p-crazy PI
I'm a hard drinkin' hard speakin' where my eggs? PI

I'm a land-based PI
I'm a fanua PI
I'm a village is the centre of my world PI

I'm a harvesting PI
a copra sacking PI
I'm a buy tinned beef 'cos no more fish in reef PI

I'm a diabetic PI
I'm a heart-diseased PI
I'm a gout-inflated, incubated, case study PI

I'm a siva Samoa PI
I'm an ava-pouring PI
I'm a tulafale tonguing genealogy PI

I'm an independent PI
I'm a flag-raisin' PI
I'm a fa'alavelave lovin' givin' livin' PI

I'm a still PI
I'm a broken PI
I'm a wheelchair bound from drunken westie driver PI

I'm a standing PI
I'm a beehive PI
I'm a labour MP gonna be PM one day PI

I'm a quiet PI
I'm a small PI
I'm a take no lunch to school today but . . . anyway PI

I'm an all-black PI
I'm an all-white PI
I'm a gold silver bronze blue street-signed PI

I'm an angry PI
I'm a dawn-raided PI
I'm a crouching poly panther in grey lynn PI

I'm a shark-toothed PI
I'm a tatau PI
I'm a malu and a pe'a, flying fox let loose PI

I know how to be in this world
I know how to feed in its waters
I know how to read the stars and sea-birds
I know how to live off poetry
I know how to give it away

I'm a propertied PI
a self-employed PI
I'm a mocha-drinkin', horn-rimmed glasses, real TV PI

I'm a movin' PI
I'm a groovin' PI
I'm a nesian mystik stratospheric whippin' it PI

I'm a krumpin' PI
a go-for-God PI
I'm a colour-free gangsta wannabe for the Lord PI

I'm a BA PI
I'm an MA PI
I'm a PhD, BCOM, LLB, MD PI

I'm a bi PI
I'm a gay PI
I'm a cross-gendered, soul-blended, mascara'd PI

I'm a coloured PI
I'm a canvassed PI
an acrylic, oil, PVC, four by two PI

I'm a bit of both PI
a chameleon PI
a hybrid, mongrelised self-satisfied PI

I'm a shadowing PI
I'm a fathoming PI
I'm an ocean, I'm the wave, I'm the depths of it PI

I'm a territorial PI
I'm a pure blood PI
I'm a border language Stop Do Not Pass Go PI

I'm a freezing works PI
I'm an IT PI
I'm a sewing, stuffing, soaking, shaking, stirring PI

I'm a talanoa PI
I'm a ta/va PI
I'm the space, the time, the tune, the transcending PI

I'm a pair of jimmy choos
I'm a size 12 in fuchsia please
I'm a no shoe fits the foot of an earth mama

I'm a royal PI
I'm a commoner PI
I'm a coup-supported, you and you and you, deported PI

I'm a white sunday PI
an LMS PI
I'm a born-again no mandatory tithing PI

I'm tihei, that first born breath
I'm that pulsating cord
I'm that breaking water
I'm that loose knot threatening to tighten

I'm that blood clot PI
that topknot PI
that loosener of sun and skin and brothers PI

I'm a lover PI
I'm a mama PI
I'm a breast-feed till they tell you *I'm done now!* PI

I'm a Nafanua PI
I'm a warrior PI
I'm the breast-kept secret in ancient samoan warfare PI

I'm a dub dub dub PI
I'm a bebo PI
I'm a good lookin', face bookin' hookin' up PI

I'm a melting pot PI
an homogenous PI
I'm a skim milk green top fat free heterogeneous PI

I'm a denny's PI
I'm a sawadee PI
I'm a finger lickin' KFC MDs BK PI

I'm a matariki PI
I'm a slammin' poetry PI
I'm a riding high and whippin' the hide of a clydesdale PI

I'm a niu FM PI
I'm a curtained stage PI
I'm a naked and I'm laughing and cartooning PI

I'm a vaka PI
I'm a star-charting PI
I'm a navigating by nissan navara PI

I'm a long poem PI
I'm a long song PI
I'm a smooth crooner softly lullabying PI

I'm a red-lipsticked PI
I'm a big-haired PI
a multi-coloured, stilhouetted fafafine PI

I'm a crying PI
I'm a laugh too loud PI
I'm a *my jandal your mouf* derek-wannabe PI

I'm a lali
I'm where we once belonged
I'm a dream fish floating
I'm wild dogs under my skirt
I'm searching for nei nim'anoa
I'm a native daughter
I'm poétes du pacifique en couleur
I'm light in the crevice never seen
I'm the girl in the moon circle

I'm niu voices
I'm songs of love
I'm mi mere
I'm houses
I'm a pinnacle
I'm a nuanua
I'm blackstone
I'm tapa talk
I'm kakala
and langakali
and hingano
I'm tai, heart of a tree
I'm colonised people
I'm praying parents
I'm a shark-skin drum
I'm solaua, a secret embryo
I'm whetu moana
I'm a young artist in contemplation
I'm the choice of your parents
I'm an act of war
I'm na buka vivinei malivi pa zinama roviana
I'm threads of a tivaevae
I'm cyclone country

I'm a theorising slot machine
bloodless coup jimmy choos
lover blood clot melting pot
shark-toothed brothers let loose
white sunday lippy BA

I'm a fast talkin' PI

ACRONYM

for Tom

When that aretalogist finished her PI poem he thought
she'd been talking about something Politically Incorrect,
like a Private Investigator looking into Penile Implant
scandals breaking International Protocol as penned by
the Istiqlal Party in Morocco and protected by Patente
de Invenção in Brazil.

But after Periodic Inspection, after taking Perpetual
Inventory of words, dragging images out from their
holes, white knuckling their tails so that the sound and
texture is wrung out of their flailing bodies, he started
getting closer. Perhaps she was from the Pacific
Institute, worked for the Pacific Internet?

Still, he wouldn't be able to find his way out of a cardboard
box filled with tiny slivers of PolyIsocyanurate, even
with the Package Insert on the Packet Interface with the
Page Interleaving in bold Page Impression stating how to
get out of the poetic Paradigm Infinitum he was faced with.

It's what happens when you get this Parallel Interface
between words and meanings. Some need clear
Parameter Identifiers, or at least a Parameter Indicator,
to know where the meaning boundaries lie, where the
'I get it' place signs are posted to stop any Paranoid
Ideation and the calling in of some poetic Paranormal
Investigator just to locate the presence of a Predictive
Index, complete with dictionary.

No. It's simply a non-hearing thing. Everyone from the
sole listener to those from Parents for Inclusion – even
with a Paternity Index revealing Partner Institutions

based on Payload Integrator (that ultimate Performance Indicator for some, but not me because I'm trying to write a poem) – should be able to see something, that thing emitted by the Pentium Intel, but there's so much Pass Interference (the poem as football) because Passes Intercepted (meaning caught) in that 'ah ha' moment, well, it's a rare thing. There are more Passive Intercepts where meaning just kind of rolls at your feet and you kick it around a little bit before booting it over the fence and smashing someone else's pink flamingo, because this meaning-maker seems Perceptually Impaired and risks Personal Injury – to the poem that is.

So if he manages to pass Phase I, he'll need to take Physical Inventory and if he still doesn't 'get it', he'd then be considered Post Intelligence, beyond Programme Instructions or any Poem Integrity. At this point, he should feel free to engage in as much Public Intoxication as he wants, because the Purchasing Instructions with this particular poem were, after all, freely available as Public Information. Unfortunately, the various practices of Protocol Interruption enacted by the Pulse Inverter nature of his enquiry has in fact, killed the poem. I told him to expect my Pro forma Invoice in the mail.

OUTCAST

for Alice

I'm a darling in the margins
but you said

be nobody's darling / be an outcast
take the contradictions of your life
and wrap around / you like a shawl
to parry the stones / to keep you warm

I keep what you said
pinned by brass tacks
against every wall 'cos

I'm a darling by nature

traitor to the rebel
show me a mould
I'll fill it, an unmade bed
I've already made it

draw me a paper road I'll sign it
over to whoever says
they need it diverted for a better cause
but you said

be nobody's darling

and that which casts me out
is cast about me
that which warms my flesh
guards my bones

and when I found
it to be true

the part about freedom
your shawl

became a fall of Huka curls
plunging black through suburban streets

a grey beach cottage firing
paua spirals under its eaves

his hand pressing want under
the wake table

a cocooning quilt pulled back under
the slim promise of sun

a brown woman walking
genealogy swimming her calves

a green dress worn on a blue blue day
because she can

it's become a map
to get us beyond the line
the justified edge
that breaking page

it's become a map in my arms
to get us beyond the reef

ACKNOWLEDGEMENTS

Fa'afetai i le Atua. Fa'afetai tele lava to my husband, David, and sons, Javan, Micah and Davey, for the daily poetry of their lives.

Alofa and appreciation to 'Gran' (Clarice Ilene Geboers née Miles), for stitching creativity and colour into my life from the very beginning; to my brother and sister, Luka Fa'amanu and Sam Lelei, for always believing, always loving; and Captain-Uncle John Glew, for nurturing a young questioning mind.

Fa'afetai tele lava to Albert Wendt for lending me a black star (and to Reina for lending me Albert). Michele Leggott: a matua tokotoko in the flesh. Taele Marsh, for patient answers to quirky questions about Samoan culture. Tim Page, for sharing his musical, multimedia talent in order to fine-tune the orality in some pieces. Also to other 'circle of stone' placeholders: Paula, Tala, Alice, Teresia, the Polynation '08 crew (Tusiata, Doug, Anya, Karlo, Serie, Daren, Mua, Tim, Kath), Sia, Sina Va'ai, Naomi Losch from Hawai'i and Strata / Translate audiences (2005-07).

Fa'afetai tele lava to Creative New Zealand for providing financial support during the initial development of this manuscript. Also many thanks to my editor, Anna Hodge, and the AUP team.

Some of these poems have appeared in *Dreadlocks in Oceania, Du Pacifique, Mana, Niu Voices, Wasafiri, Whetu Moana, Best New Zealand Poems 2006, How2* and online at Blackmail Press, Leafsalon, the New Zealand Electronic Poetry Centre (**nzepc**) and Pasifika Poetry.

NOTES

The translations below are of lesser known Samoan, Maori, Tongan, Tahitian and Hawaiian words. Except where sourced, they are personal and hence idiosyncratic.

NOT ANOTHER NAFANUA POEM
va'a: seafaring vehicle
koko alaisa: favoured Samoan dish made of rice, coconut milk and cocoa
faleuila: toilet
saka: boiled food
aiga: extended family
kalo: taro, a root plant
makeke fou: new market in central Apia
kupe: money
Vaisigano: Upolu's largest river, running through Apia
kua back: colloquial expression for the villages further most from Apia, has connotations of unsophistication

AFAKASI
afakasi: transliteration for 'half-caste', meaning part-Samoan and literally meaning half of one
va: an interrelational space between people; between people and the environment
fe'e: octopus; ancient Samoan god of war whose tentacles reached the four corners of the world and was used as a compass; often manifested in thunder
fagogo: tales
matua tausi: older woman
pouliuli: blackness, void
moko: Maori facial tattoo
fa'ataupati: Samoan clap dance performed by males
siva: Samoan dance
tau'olunga: Tongan solo dance commonly performed by unmarried women
kagamea: the Samoan practice of washing clothes, traditionally by hand on river rocks where clothes are beaten with sticks (sasa)
makeke: marketplace

CALABASH BREAKERS
Refers to the legendary Maori love story of Hinemoa
and Tutanekai

HONE SAID
See Chris Abani's Tapa Notebook at
www.nzepc.auckland.ac.nz/features/tapa/images/
notebook_abani03.jpg. Tuwhare's line actually reads
'Right now, the only Land Rights I can claim for sure –
are lodged between my toes', from *Fifteen Minutes in the
Life of Johannes H. Jean Ivanovich* in Wendt, Whaitiri and
Sullivan (eds), *Whetu Moana: Contemporary Polynesian
Poems in English* (AUP, 2003), p. 239

SONG FOR TERRY
sapasui: Samoan chop suey

CARDBOARD CROWNS
tama aiga: of kingly or high chiefly status
Tagaloa's boat builders: See *Tala o le Vavau: The Myths, Leg-
ends and Customs of Old Samoa* (Polynesian Press, 1987).

LE AMATAGA / THE BEGINNING
The title is taken from Albert Wendt's first public art
exhibition held in Honolulu, Hawai'i, August 2007.
malo lava: well done, implies the reward for hard work
ua sua mai le tai taeao / ua a'e i lagi le gogosina: these lines
appear in one of Wendt's paintings
malaga: journey
e Pele e, e Pele e, e Pele e: traditional Hawaiian refrain
chanted in addressing Pele, Hawaiian volcano deity

CIRCLE OF STONES
kakala: Tongan plants of value used in garlands, symbolic
of love and respect
heilala: sacred Tongan plant (*Garcinia sessilis*) with bright
red flowers, used in special garlands
langakali: rare tree (*Aglaia saltatorum*) bearing a highly
sirable scented flower

ta'ovala: sash (often woven) worn by Tongans as a public show of respect and formality

ipu ava: hollowed half coconut shell used for serving ava

siapo: tapa cloth

pulu: short for 'puluvao', referring to rubber tree (*Funtumia elastica*)

Nafanua: legendary Samoan goddess of war

te moana nui: short for 'te moana nui a Kiwa' ('the great ocean of Kiwa') of Maori mythology

Poutūterangi: Maori name given to the star that indicates the time of harvesting during Matariki, the Maori new year beginning in June

MUTINY ON PITCAIRN

Tēhuteatuaonoa: otherwise known as Jenny, Tahitian partner of John Adams, the last surviving mutineer from the *Bounty*. Her story appeared in the *Sydney Gazette* on 17 July 1819 and challenged the myth that women were willing, passive pawns for the mutineers. According to Pacific historian Patty O'Brien, she built a boat, planning to escape with other women, but her plans were thwarted.

TWO NUDES ON A TAHITIAN BEACH, 1894
The more common date for this painting is 1891/1894

VENUS IN TRANSIT
See Metcalfe, *Transit of Venus* (Huia Publishers, 2004).
Ma'ohi: indigenous Tahitians (Maori)
tupuna vahine: Tahitian for female ancestor

REALPOLITIK
The italicised lines were written by Cook and excerpted from Beaglehole (ed.), *The Journals of Captain James Cook on his Voyage of Discovery: The Voyage of the Resolution and Discovery, 1776–1780*, volume 1 (Cambridge, 1967).

HAS THE WHOLE TRIBE COME OUT FROM ENGLAND?
These are the names of the first settler ships to arrive in
New Zealand, mainly from England. Maori at the time,
unaware of the real terms of the settlement being nego-
tiated with the British government, and the degree and
permanency of colonial migration, were said to have
asked the question in the title. My great-great-grandfa-
ther, John Miles, was on board the *Aurora* which left
London in 1839 and arrived in Wellington, January
1840, three weeks before the signing of the Treaty.

HAWAI'I: PRELUDE TO A JOURNEY
fa'alifu fa'i: Samoan dish of green bananas cooked in
  coconut cream
hula halau: native Hawaiian dance academies
Pele-'ai-honua: Hawaiian for 'Pele, eater of the land', one
  of many names for the Hawaiian volcano deity.
  Offerings of food and money wrapped in ti or taro
  leaves continue to be made as part of indigenous
  worship of her.

FAST TALKIN' PI
fanua: land
tulafale: Samoan orator
fa'alavelave: Samoan cultural practice of reciprocal
  giving during major life events
malu: Samoan tattoo for women
pe'a: Samoan tattoo for men; flying fox

SELINA TUSITALA MARSH is of Samoan, Tuvalu, English and French descent. She was the first Pacific Islander to graduate with a PhD in English from the University of Auckland and is now a lecturer in the English Department, specialising in Pacific literature. Marsh is the coordinator of Pasifika Poetry (www.nzepc.auckland.ac.nz/ pasifika/index.asp), a sister site of the New Zealand Electronic Poetry Centre. She was involved in, and wrote the Afterword for, *Niu Voices: Contemporary Pacific Fiction 1* (2006) and is currently working on a critical anthology of first-wave Pacific women poets writing in English. Her academic and creative writing deals with issues that affect Pasifika communities in Aotearoa New Zealand and indigenous peoples elsewhere. She lives on Waiheke Island with her family.

Also available in the Arc
INTERNATIONAL POETS series

LOUIS ARMAND (Australia)
Inexorable Weather

DAVID BAKER (USA)
Treatise on Touch

ALISON CROGGON (Australia)
The Common Flesh

SARAH DAY (Australia)
New & Selected Poems

KEKI DARUWALLA (India)
The Glass-Blower: Selected Poems

GAIL DENDY (South Africa)
Painting the Bamboo Tree

ROBERT GRAY (Australia)
Lineations

MICHAEL S. HARPER (USA)
Selected Poems

SASKIA HAMILTON (USA)
Canal

ALAMGIR HASHMI (Pakistan)
The Ramazan Libation

DENNIS HASKELL (Australia)
Samuel Johnson in Marrickville

DINAH HAWKEN (New Zealand)
Small Stories of Devotion

BRIAN HENRY (USA)
Astronaut
Graft
Quarantine : Contagion

RICHARD HOWARD (USA)
Trappings

T. R. HUMMER (USA)
Bluegrass Wasteland

ANDREW JOHNSTON (New Zealand)
The Open Window
Sol

JOHN KINSELLA (Australia)
Comus: A Masque
America (A Poem)
Lightning Tree
The Silo: A Pastoral Symphony
The Undertow: New & Selected Poems
Landbridge: An Anthology of
Contemporary Australian Poetry
ED. JOHN KINSELLA

PATRICK LANE (Canada)
Syllable of Stone

ANTHONY LAWRENCE (Australia)
Strategies for Confronting Fear

THOMAS LUX (USA)
The Street of Clocks

J.D.McCLATCHY (USA)
Division of Spoils

ALVIN PANG (Singapore)
When the Barbarians Arrive

TRACY RYAN (Australia)
Hothouse

MARY JO SALTER (USA)
A Kiss in Space

ELIZABETH SMITHER (New Zealand)
A Question of Gravity

C. K. STEAD (New Zealand)
Straw into Gold
The Right Thing
Dog

ANDREW TAYLOR (Australia)
The Stone Threshold